An Inventor's Vision

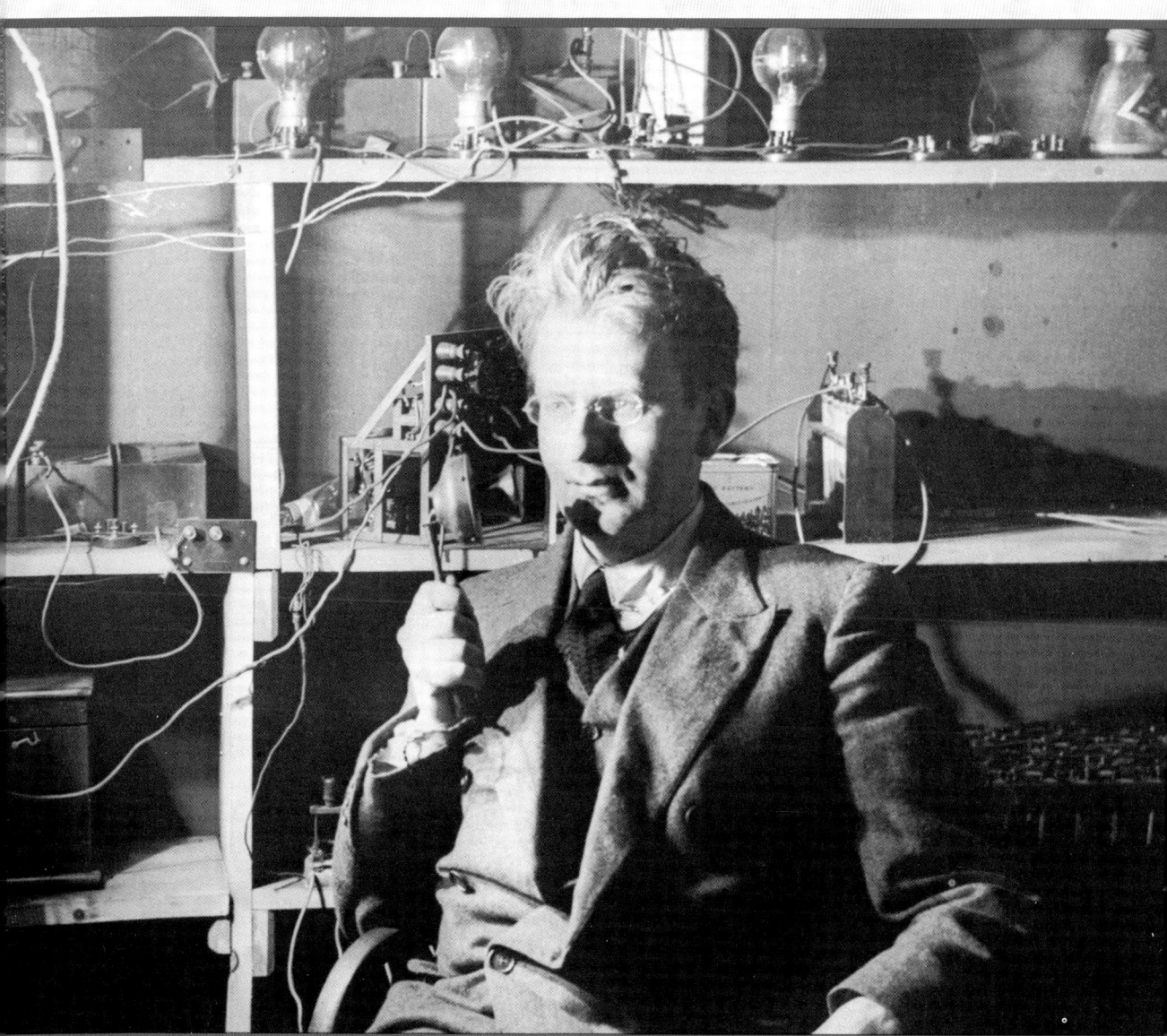

Written by Janine Scott
Illustrated by John Bennett

Contents

Who Was John Logie Baird?	4
The Boy Inventor	6
The Yearn to Learn	8
Off to the Tropics	10
The Contraption	12
A Dummy Run	14
The Televisor	16
Across the Ocean	18
Set to Take Off	20
The Vision of Television	22
What If?	24
Index	24

Who Was John Logie Baird?

John Logie Baird was an engineer and an inventor. He was also a pioneer in the development of early television. Throughout his life, he was plagued by illness and a lack of money to fund his inventions. Often he had no money to buy food or clothing because he had spent it all on equipment for his inventions.

As a child, John's poor health prevented him from going to school for weeks on end, and, later in life, to work for long periods. However, he put these times to good use. He spent hours dreaming up inventions and building contraptions. He was a determined and resourceful inventor who lived to invent. His single-mindedness and hard work led him to great achievements. This was a remarkable feat for someone who had received no scientific training at school.

1888	1914	1920	March 1925
John Logie Baird is born in Helensburgh, Scotland.	World War I prevents John from finishing his university studies.	John moves to Trinidad in the Caribbean for health reasons.	John gives the first public demonstration of the Televisor at a department store in London.

Setting the Scene

Scotland in the Early 1900s

People who lived in Scotland during this period experienced very different ways of life. It was a time when social standing in society was very important. As the son of a minister of the Church of Scotland, John Logie Baird was able to move among the upper, middle, and lower classes. However, he had little time for social rules. His mind was set on inventing things.

Few people had electricity in their homes in the early 1900s. Candles or lamps provided houses with light. People would gather around the fire, reading books and telling stories. By the 1920s, people listened to their radios for entertainment. Little did they know that television would soon bring pictures of the world into their living rooms.

May 1927	February 1928	September 1928	1946
John transmits pictures over telephone lines from England to Scotland.	John is the first to transmit pictures across the Atlantic.	The Baird Televisor goes on sale. It is the first mass-produced television set.	John Logie Baird dies of pneumonia at age 57.

The Boy Inventor

1901

John's bones ached from the cold and dampness. He had caught another chill and was home from school. He was happy though. It meant he didn't have to recite classical *Latin and Greek to his teacher. Instead, he could tinker with the telephone exchange he'd set up in his bedroom. He and four school friends had rigged up wires between their houses—around chimney pots, over gardens, and up trees.*

As John busied himself, he was unaware that his exchange would soon stop transmitting. One stormy night, a driver of a horse-drawn bus didn't see John's low-hanging wire and drove into it. It gave the man a nasty shock, throwing him to the ground. John soon got a nasty shock, too. The Helensburgh telephone company made John take apart his illegal telephone exchange, but that didn't dampen this Scottish boy's inventing spirit.

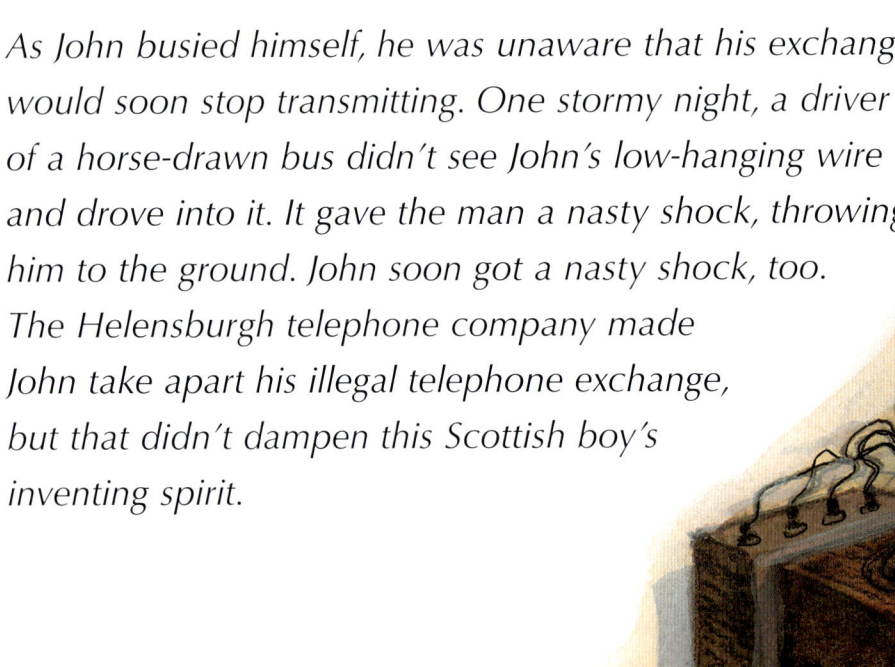

classical relating to ancient art, literature, or culture

> "There is nothing like a classical education to turn a boy's mind into really practical channels."
> —John Logie Baird

John's passion for inventions started to take shape in 1900. He and his friend Godfrey Harris designed a glider and took it up on the roof of John's house. As John fiddled with the controls, Godfrey suddenly pushed the aircraft off the roof. The glider broke in half, and John fell to the ground. Even this disaster did not stop him. John went on to supply his house with electricity at a time when others in Helensburgh were still using candles.

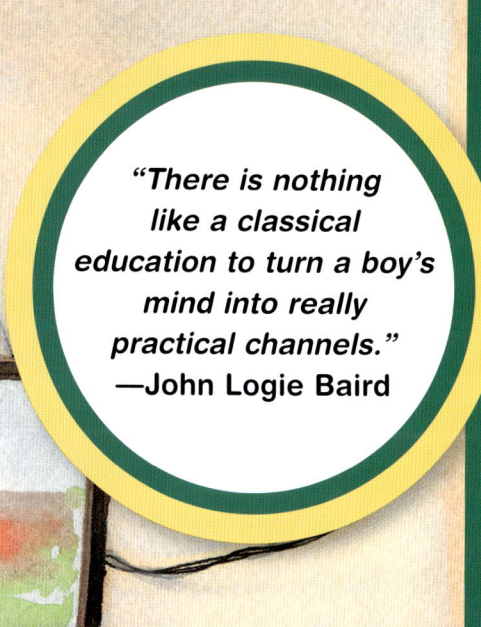

John took this photograph of his home, *The Lodge*. When John was a young boy, he invented a remote-control device for his camera. It allowed him to take photographs of himself, even while he slept!

The Yearn to Learn

1905

John was happiest doing experiments in the kitchen of The Lodge, even when he burned his fingers and filled the house with smoke! His parents had set their hearts on John becoming a church minister, but they soon realized that this was not the life for their inventor son. Therefore, they gave their permission for him to study electrical engineering. It took John eight long years to graduate because he was often too ill to attend classes.

Later on, John's efforts to study for a degree in science were cut short by World War I. He became an assistant engineer for an electrical company, but emergency call-outs on cold, wet nights forced him to his sick bed for weeks on end. Even when John was called up to fight for his country, his poor health let him down once again. The doctor stamped his file "unfit for any service." John's war work took place in peaceful Helensburgh.

During John's three years at the electrical company, he was always coming up with ideas for inventions. Inspired by H. G. Wells's book *The Diamond Maker*, John first tried to manufacture diamonds at work. The experiment ended with a huge power outage in the area.

Another venture was more successful. John suffered from cold feet, so he turned his problem into a thriving sock business. He sprinkled borax powder, which absorbed moisture, onto the socks. However, the buyers didn't know that when they washed them, the borax was washed away!

The Baird Undersock was sold to stores and advertised on sandwich boards. Women, rather than men and boys, carried the sandwich boards. This was unusual for the time, but it was typical of John to invent such an innovative marketing plan.

Off to the Tropics

1920

John lay in bed, shivering under the blankets. The cold, wet Scottish climate had made him ill again. In an attempt to restore his health, he decided to move to the Caribbean island of Trinidad. After three weeks on a ship and then one week recovering from illness, John launched yet another money-making scheme. It seemed like the most obvious business venture in a land of sugar plantations and fruit trees. He would make and sell guava jelly, mango chutney, and orange marmalade.

By night, John found time for his scientific inventions. However, the locals didn't understand his work and were fearful of the goings-on. One night, the flashes of light and noises of John's experiments stirred up trouble. Out of fear, the locals threw mud and grass at John, but nothing could deter him from inventing. He simply threw the mud and grass back at them!

deter to stop or prevent

> "The only progress I made in that West Indies year was toward television. I spent my nights in the jungle working out problems."
> —John Logie Baird

John's jelly making in Trinidad was a success—at least with the island's insects! The sweet smell attracted swarms of bugs. Wasps and bees ended up floating in the preserves, and ants raided the sugar supplies.

To make things worse, John caught malaria, a disease transmitted by mosquitoes. In October 1920, poor health forced him back to London. He brought his unsold preserves, but no one was interested in buying any, so he ended up selling the whole lot to a sausage-maker for next to nothing.

John's jelly factory was housed in a lean-to beside his hut. He mixed his preserves in a large copper washtub and then cooked them over a brick fireplace with a chimney.

The Contraption

1923

Upon his return to Britain, John spent the first few weeks sick in bed, dreaming up ways to make his fortune. When his health improved, he sold a range of products, from two tons of Australian honey to soap that he named "Baird's Speedy Cleaner." However, his trading ventures were always ruined by his poor health, so he turned his mind to inventing. He wanted to design a machine that could transmit moving pictures by wireless signals.

With little money, John had to search around junk stores and scrap yards for materials. His first "seeing wireless" was made out of a tea chest, a tin cookie jar, the lid of a hatbox, a knitting needle, a motor from an electric fan, many flashlight batteries, and other bits and pieces. The equipment ended up banging and flashing, and John's landlord threw him out of his lodgings. But for John, it was just the beginning.

wireless   a radio receiving set

While recovering from illness, John experimented with a glass safety razor that would never go blunt. He gave up on the idea, however, when he cut himself very badly. Only then did he turn his attentions to inventing a machine that transmitted moving pictures by wireless signals. His sister Annie thought he would have more success with the razor!

Poor health caused John to move to Hastings, England. It was here, while on a walk along the cliff tops to the east of Hastings, that he invented the entire system for transmitting moving pictures. He excitedly told his friend Guy "Mephy" Robertson (left) about it. His friend suggested that John stick to selling soap!

A Dummy Run

1925

A small breakthrough took place in March. The owner of a large London department store had heard of John's invention. Thinking that it would be a good store attraction, he hired John to demonstrate his machine for three weeks. Many shoppers were fascinated by the simple mask shape that appeared. Some, however, were suspicious of it, thinking it might be able to see through walls into their homes!

After the demonstration, John worked even harder. He knew that scientists with money and equipment in America were working hard on similar inventions. With a **ventriloquist's** dummy called Stooky Bill as his subject, John finally succeeded in transmitting a sharper picture that showed light and shade. Excitedly, he ran downstairs to grab a real model. He convinced an office worker to sit in front of the hot lights. As a test, John asked him to poke out his tongue. John was overjoyed when the transmitted picture poked out its tongue, too!

ventriloquist a person who produces sounds or voices that seem to come from another source

John is holding the original Stooky Bill in his right hand. He used ventriloquist's dummies during his early experiments, because they could withstand the heat and light from the lamps. A person could not have lasted for long.

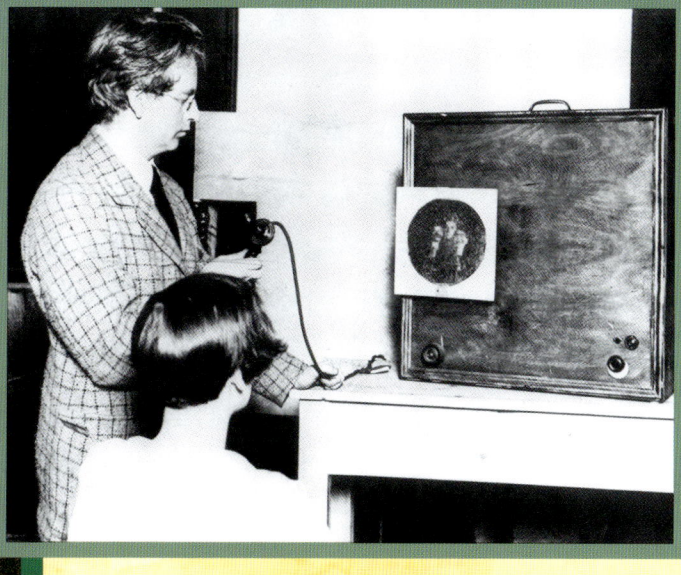

The Televisor

January 1926

More than forty guests, in batches of six, crammed into John's two attic rooms. They looked at the great jumble of wires and bits and pieces of the Televisor, the name that John had given the apparatus. Then they watched as pictures of Stooky Bill were transmitted from one room to another. The images were sometimes blurry, faint, and flickering, but the audience was impressed. Some people even took turns being on television.

A reporter wrote an article about John and his Televisor. Soon journalists as far away as America were writing about it, too. John was becoming famous on both sides of the Atlantic, but there was no time to rest. John began work on his next challenge—to transmit pictures over a greater distance.

"One of the visitors who was being transmitted had a long, white beard, part of which blew into the wheel. He was a thorough sportsman and took the accident in good part."
—John Logie Baird

The black-and-white images had tones and detail. John worked hard to make the transmitted images clearer. At times, the images flickered badly. However, John noticed that the more the images flickered, the more detail there was.

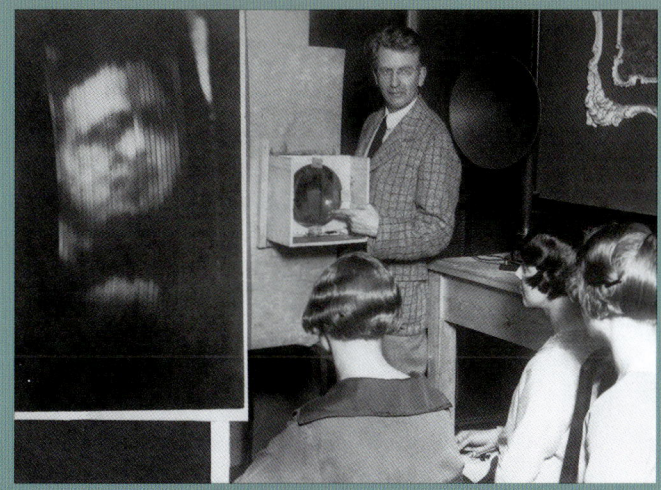

John called the receiving end of his apparatus the Televisor. The image of the face (inset above) is the first photograph of a television image.

Across the Ocean

May 1927

With the help of two people, John succeeded in sending pictures from England to Scotland. To prove there was no trickery involved, the office worker was given instructions over the telephone that he had to follow. The model and his transmitted image moved their heads on command.

Nine months later, John's friend, Oliver Hutchinson, sailed to America, taking with him a television receiver. The first attempt to send pictures across the Atlantic failed on February 7, but John was not discouraged. The next night, he tried again with the help of experts. This time, the pictures traveled 3,500 miles to an astonished audience. John made headlines once again. His achievement was now being recognized in America.

John wanted to be the first person to send a picture message across the Atlantic, just as in 1901 Guglielmo Marconi, an Italian inventor and electrical engineer, had been the first person to send a transatlantic radio message. The two men shared a common bond. They both devoted their lives to their inventions.

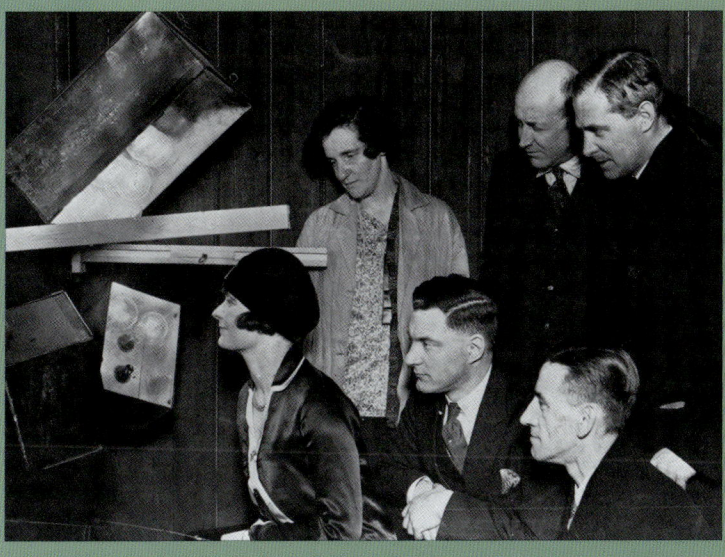

John applied for and received a transmitting license from the post office. The transmitter helped John broadcast the first picture message across the Atlantic. At first, pictures of Stooky Bill were sent. Then John sent images of himself. Mia Howe (above) was the first woman to have her image transmitted from London to New York.

Set to Take Off

1928

An inventor never stops inventing. John thought the world was now ready for television sets. So, at the Radio Exhibition in Olympia, London, Baird Televisors went on sale. Famous for his ingenious marketing ideas, John even persuaded some famous actors who were visiting the show to make impromptu performances. The plan worked. His Televisor sets received a great deal of free publicity.

By the next year, the Baird Televisors were mass-produced. An engineer who had also been at the exhibition made a metal model set to replace John's bulky wooden prototypes. The company the man worked for won the contract to make the sets. The Baird Televisor became the world's first mass-produced television set. Television was now set to change the world forever!

prototype an original model of an invention

Three models of Televisors went on sale at Olympia. John was not allowed to do demonstrations for the Televisors in the main radio exhibition hall. People had to leave the hall and go across the street!

John Logie Baird's television set, the Baird Televisor, was first mass-produced by the Plessey Company. About 1,000 sets were made and sold between 1929 and 1931.

The Vision of Television

John Logie Baird's work was a well-kept secret. He fiercely guarded the workings of his machine, because he realized that people working on similar inventions might use his pioneering work in television for their own advantage.

John worked long hours alone. At times, he had technicians help him make components for the apparatus, but they always worked in isolation. Only John knew how all the pieces fit together. When he gave demonstrations, it was not uncommon for John to hide parts of the machine or to demonstrate earlier models so that onlookers could not see his latest models.

John was racing against time. Many others, with more money and more equipment, were working hard, too. However, John Logie Baird's determination to succeed helped him become a leader in television technology.

component   a part of a machine

Leading the Way

John Logie Baird had many firsts in television. In 1928, he transmitted color television pictures and demonstrated his 3-D television. He was also the first to broadcast live scenes outside, using a camera mounted in a van.

The desire for both himself and for Scotland to be first in this new technology led John Logie Baird to demonstrate his inventions as soon as he knew they would work. They were often very crude examples of what could be achieved.

Fortunately, John patented some of his work. A patent is a license for the right to make, use, and sell an invention. It lasts for a set period of time. Through patents, inventors have long protected their original ideas and inventions.

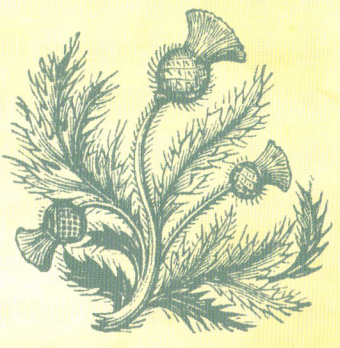

What If?

John Logie Baird's own country was his toughest critic. Some scientists even wondered if there was trickery involved in his inventions. In the end, John became more famous in America. What if John Logie Baird had listened to critics and had become discouraged?

John had to be very resourceful, using equipment found in scrap yards. What might John have achieved if he had received the funding that other scientists often had? What might have happened if he had let illness stand in the way of his dream and vision?

How can we show commitment in our everyday lives?

Index

Helensburgh	4–8
patents	23
Radio Exhibition	20–21
Stooky Bill	14–16, 19
Televisors	5, 16–17, 20–21
Transatlantic	5, 18–19
Trinidad	4, 10–11

commitment being involved wholeheartedly